sing pilgrimage
and exile

murray bodo

*"Francis wished that all things
should sing pilgrimage and exile."*
– *Thomas of Celano*

Cover and book design by John Quigley, O.F.M.
SBN 0-912228-71-7
© 1980 St. Anthony Messenger Press
Printed in the U.S.A.

CONTENTS

I. four loves

To Donald M. Murray

INNER SEARCHES

Like the cobweb patterns
of Rand McNally road maps
journeys are weaving paths
through my wrinkled life,
veining me and creasing me.

FATHER

I've searched for you, my Father,
down the seasons of my years,
and all the pain and sterile tears
are somehow bringing you
to birth within me. You, my Father,
are my son; in this new birth your
fatherhood is mine forever.

SONG FOR CHRIST JESUS

I sing of sagebrush and cedar
and stars I watched by night.

I bring them to you again
dusted with desert living
and lay my weary head
upon your shoulder white.

And then the sagebrush fills
my nostrils, and memory quickens
to those hills and cedar trees
beneath whose twisted limbs
you found me, a boy becoming.

All my loves, licit though they are,
some star sees; the sweet cedar
fills my brain and I remember you.
The song of sage sounds again,
and I look up into starless clouds
loud with your hiding.

I hear the wind whine through cedar,
stars shine again in my mind;
sage floats in the fragrant air,
and you merge into silver,
my heart rising, remembering
the way it is with you and me,
sensing the way it will be.

HOLY SPIRIT

Standing at my sink
the other day,
watching soapy water
swirl dirt down the drain,
I thought of everything
that was washing away
and of you, and of how,
Pentecostally, you slip
through my life
like shampoo suds
leaving clean brown hair
and bright brow behind.

VISITATION

a white-tailed doe
arcing with natural motion
over the mountain snow

Mary of Nazareth
riding with virgin devotion
the hills to Elizabeth

ADVENT SKY

this gray-white day
    away from you
a pencil-stroked horizon
dull silver birch-spray
    of branches caught through
    silent spaces on one hue
wrought-iron blue

PILGRIM'S CHRISTMAS

Years on the road, Lord,
hoarding this gift
stored within my heart,
fearful
of not sighting the star again,
biffing across
this desert of mine:
panic-stricken mind
filled with visions of sand dunes
surrounding me,
blocking my way to you,
lost
in a circle of sand
with my gift glassed up inside,
until
you sent your star to lead me

out of this world of sand,
knowing
as you did,
that no one finds the road to Bethlehem
in a sand cone
but only
in the free, mystic act
of looking
up and out,
breaking the spiral, and . . .
Ah, heart, now offer
heart-gift,
sieze compass light, and . . .
and . . .
Look out for circles,
won't you?

THIRD FLOOR ROOM *me too!*

I am sitting at evening in a room
in my old theology house, that white study
where I prepared for ordination.
It is fifteen years since I left
the silence of these cream-colored corridors
and drove stealthily away to what I hoped
would and must be better.
And now back here alone
hearing again the sound of
my own vacuous thoughts
rattling around this small cell,
I wonder about the years
and what they can mean
when counted backwards
to the source that made them.
(Or was it this future that made them?)
I know now that it wasn't

this place that made the years good
but what happened to me
because I sat four years
in this unpainted room.
I lost my balance and found it again
in the same blankness of white.
I found something in me that
could paint this room any color,
and remembering that
has made the whole projection
of my life a thrust of paint
onto anything that threatens
to become a dull, flat white.
Life asks me to color it bright,
and I draw upon this room
to find a reason why I should.

WINTER DAY

an edge of snow
   on my buried-seed days
   and white boredom
smothering my clogged pores

my dried roots and stem
   reach out
   timidly
   for someone
above or below the dark
   but I only touch again
   the barren thigh of winter

I wait once more for May
   to coax my green shoots out
   trembling
for fear no one will be there
   forever

WINTER

Mary of Nazareth,
like snow falling
swiftly,
secretly
upon the passive earth,
you cover us
with white warmth,
burrowing under your drifts,
bear-like
in our hibernation
from the heart's stormy season.

WINTER BIRDS

The gray of winter
charcoals the horizon
outside my window,
and I notice
more crows on wing
above our neighbor's
barn. Gray does
bring out crows
and seems to soot
all winging creatures.
Even harmless chickadees
that dot the landscape
and clutter up
the long straight lines
of aging birch branches
seem sinister
on a gray day
in February.

OLD JACKET

This old jacket
has seen me
through my seasons
for twenty years now.
I should pack it
up and free
myself of reasons
for remembering how
it was other winters.

OBSERVATION

A man
does
what he can,
is
what he does,
loses
what he can
not do
or be.

JEREMIAH

Before I formed you in the womb I knew you.

And who could tell the wonder of it,
who would understand?

Before you came to birth I consecrated you.

And who would have known then,
who could have told?

I have appointed you as prophet to the nations.

And who would listen,
who would not have laughed?

All this and more, pressed down and stored up
for me
in God.
All this and more stored up
for you
in God.
Come with me, and I will show you love
in the way you walk and talk
and move your eyes when you are
afraid.
Come inside and see that place in your heart

swept clean and fresh for you and God to talk
from midnight till the last drops of wax
run down onto the table top.

Do not say, "I am a Child!"

No, or I'll not
take you seriously again. When I take you
by the hand, it is to befriend you,
not to lead you like a child
to that red and white popcorn stand
where Roy Rogers waits in the dark room
that enters to the left.
O, do not say you are little
any more.
Into your delicate mouth I am putting words
that will harden the lips and set firm your jaw
for prophesying
and proclaiming oracles.

Day after day until his dying day.

I heard your voice and
the choice was clear
once, for all, definite,
unmistaken, ringing,
ringing, ringing in my ear.

HAWKS

Two red-tails screaming above me
wringing my neck upwards to the sky
where one lone plane pulls a glider
against the tug of gravity.
And I yearn to be pulled high
above myself, to be a rider
behind a plane about to free me
for a soar in space soft as eider.

PARTING

It was in the way
you said, "good-bye"
that I saw why
you couldn't stay.
It will be the cry
of another day
will make you say,
"I didn't try."

DISTRACTION

While you were here,
I forgot to keep things orderly
and dust settled
on my desk again.
Then when you left
so suddenly,
I couldn't bring myself
to dust the room.

"THE INEXTINGUISHABLE"
for Carl Nielsen

White bones bathed
in white moon,
naked on dune
dust, swathed
in lunar beams

But I . . .

their dreams
bare and unfulfilled,
empty fields untilled
dry streams,
thirsty land

But I am . . .

battle stations manned
with skeletons of boys,
all the tinker toys
of generals canned
on color tv

For I am the . . .

boy bones free
swing in the wind
with medals pinned
to the dead tree
of their hanging

But I am the Resurrection

kettle drums banging
their victory song,
trumpets blasting strong,
bone bells clanging

That I am the Resurrection the Life

allegro
poco allegretto
poco adagio quasi andante!

I am the Resurrection

allegro, the Life,
allegro, forever,
allegro, allegro . . .

REQUIEM FOR GUS

hearing this old jeep cough
and miss, I think of you
and what you'd say that I
ran out of gas, and plunged
into a ditch, and broke
the right turn signal
against a sapling oak
because I couldn't think
or act, hearing of your
dark coma suddenly and
without warning, and I
lean on this steering
wheel turned away
from that future road
and weep for you who
made me laugh in this
same jeep when both its
signal lights were working

BIRDS FLYING SOUTH

Blackbirds flying south
in little black bundles,
rain clouds gathering . . . .
It is the eve
of the Feast of St. Francis.
I rise
and fly south to the sun
in one of those tight knots
of birds,
togethering it with them,
fleeing from cold
and wet
on hopeful wings,
with wind
cutting little wrinkles
at the corners
of my eyes.
I go with you, little birds.
You have taken my heart's eyes
while I sit in the wet woods,
blind,
listening for the silence
of escaping feathers to float
above me.

VIEWS FROM MY WINDOW

I.

A soft rain falls outside my window and the maple tree across the drive looks for all its golden beauty forlorn and ready to lose the last of its leaves. I think it was raining the day I discovered you, Francis. At least it was autumn and a driving wind forced me into the school library to escape the melancholy sound of fall. I can still see the little book standing on the shelf, and the little flowers around the edges; but I don't remember who wrote it or what the title was. I think it was simply, *Francis of Assisi.* I have often thought of going back to that little room and trying to re-create that discovery just as it was so long ago. But the school has burned to the ground now, and all the books with it. And perhaps that is good for me, the burning of attachments and mementos, even of you, Father Francis.

It was there in that little public school library that I realized not so much your joy, Francis, as my own emptiness and lack of everything you possessed in having nothing. There it began, the void, the nothingness that had to be filled and that only your challenge could fill. I saw in you a way to peace and joy, and that way was Christ in his poverty, Christ in his emptying.

The rest is history now. Leaving home at fourteen, the long journey from New Mexico to Ohio, the years of study, the habit, the vows, ordination. Only—through it all and even now, you still haunt me, Francis. Sometimes I see your face behind the glass of department stores and around corners, watching me, calling me out toward you, and toward some goal, some dream I haven't yet caught. You, always you, like some phantom of my own dreaming, suddenly flashing across my mind—a shadow of that face I met reading a book in the corner of a library when I was thirteen years old.

II.

The rain outside has turned to snow. What are you saying now, Father, in the coldness of that November sign of winter coming once again? It is a wet snow with nothing sticking to the ground, but the sky has become almost black to match the blackness of tree trunks across the landscape. And in this austere and damp afternoon your face again appears, Francis, laced with the slender black branches of winter's early coming. And the winter of your life is etched firmly in my mind; those black days when what you tried so hard to achieve among the brothers seemed threatened by practicalities and growing numbers, by Church laws and mediocrity and a loss of the original vision. And the darkness of winter fell upon the bright Camelot of the beginning when you and Leo and Masseo and the others charged about the countryside proclaiming your knighthood, unafraid and filled with love.

III.

Often when I look out my second-floor window in the late fall, I think of you in your sickness before the great dawn of your conversion. I think of the late, late days of your life when autumn fell from the mountains and threatened to plunge you once again into the despair of those long days when you lay in bed puffing out your lips, exhausting the spirit of all your young days on empty walls. And the low-hanging clouds seem to settle heavily on the green woods and the black branches of leafless trees, like all the threats upon the brotherhood.

IV.

Winter is settling down on my small room now. A soft mist is alternating from snow to drizzle. The trees are taking on that black, charcoal color that is a part of my memories of this seminary when I was a boy of 14. On days like this I would snuggle up in a corner of the library with a good book and hope that all the bright fluorescent lights of the world would keep out the darkness I feared. But today, Francis, so many years after, I walk out in our woods on a day like this. Somewhere along those years with you my quest drove me inward towards that darkness I so feared. And in the encounter there at the core of my own fear I broke through something to a new and hitherto hidden center of my heart where all was light and hope, where I found a small warm flame to keep me from the cold and dark and where I knew I could flee if necessary. But always in my journeys back to that small but infinite space within, I have to pass through the dark of which this day reminds me. And always it is frightening and panic-filled because of the gnawing suspicion that the flame will not be there. Perhaps that is what you felt during those long days in the cave outside Assisi when you feared the light of day and scurried off to hide in a deep cavern where any light at all had to come from within your own heart. And you persevered, didn't you, until you were sure that the flame was real?

V.

The view from my window this morning is one of those bright winter days when everything stands out in sharp detail, when the blue of the sky brightens the bare black trees and coats their sun-sides with a silver sheen. The contrast of black and silver against the blue backdrop reminds me again of your Lady Poverty. It was she who shone so brightly on the austere deprivation of your life and by some strange alchemy turned to silver the crude ore you extracted from the bowels of your world. Those black trees that looked so ominous when the rain was falling outside my window are now transparent with that radiance which is the gift of a day like this. And that glory does not come from within but is projected from the sun through blue sky like a fine white sand transforming but not obliterating the somber landscape of my window world. I would not have noticed the silver out there were it not for the stark black trees that first affronted me when all the leaves were gone.

You fought so hard, Francis, for your Lady Poverty, knowing that only she would bring lustre to the plainness of your brotherhood. As long as her countenance shone on the brotherhood, they would take something of her bright light and reflect it, mirroring her beauty to the world.

VI.

This rainy morning's darkness that grows darker as the sun rises invisibly behind the unbroken layers of wet clouds reminds me again, Francis, of the need for light. How very much of joy and love are cut off from us when we let the darkness outside overcome the light that burns within our hearts. The lights of the cars that dully burn past my window in this noon-day darkness make no impression on the gray that is not night. Something more than candle power is needed to light the way for the listless eyes of morning computers.

VII.

Something in that white birch's swaying makes this morning's view new for me. I had never really looked far enough toward the sun's rising to see it. And yet like you, Francis, it has always been there behind that little lip of windowsill I never bothered to look around. Even though the view from my window is already limited and confined to the span of my own horizon, I find myself drawing together even more compactly what I want to see. And soon I'm looking only at what I expect to see when I roll up my shades in the morning. Certain features in the landscape I single out and emphasize—as I do with your life and Rule. It wasn't till I moved to another floor and looked outside from another angle that I saw a birch tree trembling in the wind. From what new height and angle should I now view you, Father Francis? Perhaps in that ragged little sparrow swaying in the birch tree I will catch on wing some fleeting glimpse of the Little Poor Man, the poet and mystic, the saint that you are.

FOUR LOVES

I. Puppy Love

Love is
a bicycle-built-for-two
going from Chicago
to Timbuctoo.
Love is
a bicycle-built-for-two
left in a gulley
in Timbuctoo.

II. Teen Love

Love is
two straws in a chocolate shake,
one with lipstick stain
and the other plain.
Love is
two straws in an empty shake,

one with lipstick stain
and the other plain.

III. Married Love

Love is
the bicycle-built-for-two
and Timbuctoo,
and the milkshake, too,
and you.

IV. Celibate Love

Love is
a man on a tree
giving me
the cycle-for-two,
Timbuctoo,
the milkshake, too.
But not you.

RYE BEACH

I returned to the snaking beaches of Rye
and walked on the sand again.
I guess I was looking for some reason why
our Eden days were possible then.
I hoped to find you there and feel
you present beside me once more,
but the beach was hard and the reel
of gulls wound into my self's core
a loneliness that made me lie
face down on the gray beach
with the tide creeping toward my
soles, open to its hissing reach.
I had to rise and dive into the sea
before the tide came in and covered me.

BOAT RIDE

The River Charles by twilight
is not the way Romantic poets
said it would be. I might
have thought it was only me
had I not seen behind me
two young lovers intertwined,
physically turned in, with eyes
profoundly sad, looking out
upon the river passing darkly by.
What was it about the river
that reflected in their eyes
a blank that made me shiver
and wonder why two hearts
so close could be so far apart
that even I, alone, felt
closer to them than they did
to one another? I saw
then in the river a sad
symbol of their love: a dark
flowing under them, unstable,
momentary, occasional, like
a River Charles boat ride.

ITALIAN SUITE

I. Turin

Standing in the rain
under your umbrella,
I remembered Hemingway's
"Cat in the Rain,"
as we watched Turin flood
with water from the hill
we stood on, watching
Turin flood
under your umbrella.

II. Florence

All I remember of that apartment
on the Via dei Veluti is your cat.
You had removed its claws bent
on removing me where I sat at
your table eating a boiled artichoke.

And when I awoke each morning,
that clawless monster sat brooding
on its haunches eyeing me, wishing
for claws, and I would spring
from my kitchen cot, snarl back
and stalk into the bathroom where

even the bathtub was lined
with litter green.

Elizabeth and Robert Browning
used to live right around the corner,
and I wondered did they have a cat, too?

III. Pisa

Florence without the Ponte Vecchio
Florence without Michelangelo
Florence without the dough
it takes to build a real duomo.
Florence without the green glow
of eyes in your window, O
cat eyes above the Arno.

IV. Venice

I couldn't find Harry's Bar
in Venice, and I thought
maybe it had already sunk
into the sea, being less
substantial and frailer
than St. Mark's Cathedral.
And then I saw St. Mark's
sinking into the sea.

They say Harry's Bar
is going strong. It's lighter
and will probably float forever
in the cat-backed fog.

V. Reprieve

Everywhere I traveled
in Italy,
I aways ended up
in Florence,
avoiding that cat
without the claws
in that apartment
on the Via dei Velluti.

HOMEWARD BOUND

heaving sheets of rain
   slapping my windshield
bright oncoming headlights
   blinding my vision
sixty miles an hour
   splashing toward home
watching pairs of lights
   pass me by
securely in a shroud
   of white
      flickering
      mist

NOTES FOR A WATER SUITE

the staccato pulse along my heart
   crescendoing
as I drop onto the Albuquerque runway

the parched feeling along the throat
   the dry
     the acid taste of pent-up phlegm
the need for a plunge

vacation time

the trip to the desert lakes
   and the first splash of my sinkers
     into the trout-rich water
and the first light tug
   and the bobber sucked down
with that firm sliding stroke
   that massages the arm

            of my mind
straightening
   and pulling
        each tangled, clotted vein

the accelerator pressure on my sole
   and the long winding drive
        through the mountains
and the swollen clouds
   menacing the peaks
and final release of rain
   upon my balding head

I cup my hands over my ears, listening
   to the brass notes
        of Handel's Water Music
my own pulse counterpointing
   the rhythm of the rain

SING PILGRIMAGE AND EXILE

And I
pilgrim and stranger,
winging across the sky,
singing the exile
of my years

And I
trying to smile
facing the danger,
denying the tears
of waving good-bye

And I
moving swiftly
from safe geography,
tearing the garment
of the familiar

The phone is dialed
official letters sent
calling me from Ur

fashioning me
who I am
exiled brother of Assisi
son of Abraham

SPARROW

And through all my loves
and searches, in every season
and weather of my soul,
behind the faces of the men
and women I love,
and after every journey
away from you, Lord Jesus,
I find you once again.
I return and see your face
still shadowed there
beneath the lake that
lies so coolly clear
below my window.
I feel your warm love
along the length and
breadth of me and
I sigh and wonder why
you're always here
to greet me and let
my crumpled
ragged sparrow limbs
nest again with you.

II. blessingway

Blessingway is the most sacred of all the Navajo Chantways. It is concerned with restoring peace and harmony. These poems are each a diminutive Blessingway; they attempt to establish a single acre of peace against the turmoil of life.

To Daniel Kiefer

WALLS

There are no graffiti
on these walls.
And the words
I don't see
and the pictures
no one drew
leap out at me
because I thought
they would be there.
How strange.
Those blank surfaces
are smothered
by words and images
we'd try so hard
to erase
were they really there.

CROW

Not to seek to go with you,
black bird,
as you climb away from here
is sometimes
too great a pressure upon the heart,

And we succumb to wishing
we were you,
come here to rest upon some tree
and then, wordless,
wing away
to anywhere that is apart.

NIGHT HIKE

Once along the scouting trail
of my thirteenth autumn
in a September travail
of boyish bravado,
I tried to scare some
younger scouts incommunicado
as they stalked feet bound
along a path that wound
their night patrol around
the curve of my newly found
adolescence. I leapt
upon them, wildly screaming
my secrets into the kept
dark of boyhood, beaming
for joy as I lost inept
balance and crazily stepped
over the sharp cliff's edge
through the black lake's edge
into deep water.

CHILDHOOD HOME

this gray stucco house
with the glassed front porch
and the mini-plot of grass
(a brief skirt against the sand
creeping down from the hills)

I used to play here

NEW MEXICO

Out here you live
with things that are worn.
Maybe it's the wind
that makes all wheels
wagon wheels wound
round with mesquite
and leaning crazily
against old fence posts.

SAND SONNET

Feeling this long cold wind
blowing through my brain
scattering scraps of memory
over the desert where
I spent my boyhood years,
I shiver at the indecisions
that have driven me away
from the slow sands of youth.
So often, not knowing how one non-
position leads to another, we drift
like the sand and find ourselves
uprooted, afar, and afraid.
And the wind of the mind
blows erratically on.

ROOM, SWEPT AND CLEAN

When, in this abandoned cell
you try to sleep or wake or even dwell
unnoticed, the rush of wind departing
turns you out of doors and you smell
the free scent of pine needles darting
short messages of escape, and you yell.

SPIRIT WITHIN ME

down the longest syllable
        of you
            in the narrow tunnel
        of voice
under the roof of resonance
        I hear you
        vibrating
        life
plucking me into response
        and I tremble

THE WIDOW'S SON

He was a boy who lived in a small house by the
   ocean.
He loved his home on the cliff with the pounding
   of the surf below and salt spray in the air he
   breathed.
He loved his mother with her large eyes and her
   strong hands upon his shoulders.
And besides these loves there was his fascination
   for the sea, for a ride on the crest of a wave.

The boy's mother worked in the village on the
   opposite side of the cliff where the boy
   dreamed of the sea.
She trusted her boy and she trusted the barriers
   that shielded him from the waves that
   thumped on the rocks below.
But boys find ways of fulfilling their desires.

Every day when his mother was working in the
   village, the boy would hazard another barrier,
   subdue it, and advance ever closer to the
   mystic rhythm of salt water caressing the
   shore.
His mother never dreamed he was doing these
   things when she came home tired, and he
   looked at her with his large brown eyes and
   loved her.
Nor did the mother ever take her boy to the

seashore, to a quiet lagoon where he could
learn to swim.
She knew little of the sea or how to teach a boy to
swim.
The boy often wondered where his father was
and if he would have piggy-backed his son to
the seashore and eased him into shallow water
when the tide was out.
But there was no father, and the boy grew more
brazen and less cautious in his response to the
call of the sea.

Then one day the boy reached the bottom of the
rocks and stood facing the sea with his large
brown eyes.
He undressed and jumped into the shallow water
and let the waves play with him.
But the boy was not glad now.
He knew his mother would be sad to find him
there.
Yet somehow he continued to play, half at ease,
hypnotized by the water.
He played all through the heat of the afternoon.

There were many strange things on the sandy
shore, crabs, and crayfish and shells of all
colors.
From time to time gulls would dive and skim the

water, and ships would glide by on the
horizon.
How wonderful the gulls and ships were.
The gulls were greater than the ocean.
They soared high above it in the freedom of the
sky and dipped only for food.
The boy wished he were a gull and could soar
above the water.
The ships, too, were great but not greater than
the sea.
For his mother had told him of the anger of the
sea, how it could swallow up the ships and
their people, or crash them against the rocks.

His mother . . . Yes, she would be returning soon.
He must leave the salt spray now.
The boy dried in the sun awhile.
    Then he dressed and started to climb the rocks.
But he could not find the path again.
He looked hard for something to hoist him up the
first steep rocks.
But there was nothing but sand and water around
him.

Fear now seized the boy's heart, and he turned
towards the sea where the sun was floating like
a helpless orange marshmallow.
Already the tide was creeping in, and the once
friendly waves were growing larger and
hissing at him.
The boy screamed.

But no one seemed to hear above the sea's own
  insidious gasps.
He ran along the beach trying to find some rock
  to climb onto.
And the water grew higher and more shrill and
  the salt spray whipped at the boy.

He was surrounded by water now,
And the boy knew that in a few minutes he
  would be swept off his feet and carried out to
  sea.
He made one last desperate plunge through the
  water,
And stretched out his hands for something,
  anything to cling to.
And his hand met the warm hand of a fisherman
  reaching down to him . . . .

The moon was out now.
And as the woman walked up the steep grade to
  her cottage,
she saw a man coming down the road toward her,
  a fisherman on his way to the sea for a night's
  catch.
They greeted each other on the road and passed
  by.
The woman could now see the cottage and the
  smoke rising from the chimney.
She knew her boy would be waiting for her,
And she was glad for he was the only son of his
  mother.

STORM AT SEA

After the catch in the throat
that signaled terror at your leaving
and the wild poundings against the boat,
after fearing the walk upon the waters, heaving
the salty seas waves' invitation to float,
you came inside and silently grieving
with me, pretended not to note
my cowardice and non-believing.

NAVAJOLAND

Here between the maybes of the future,
I fasten upon the certainty
of landscape,
the assurance of distance from your threats
that magnified fear
to escape proportions.
The desert lies about me
and sand settles beneath my fingernails.

I wait.

I wait for the sudden tree to shade me
from what constantly assails
my peeling head.
Anxiously,
I fix my eyes
upon this desert place of refuge,
far from the dull sky
that fogged joy from your face
and left me searching for you
once too often
till I ran for deliverance.

DESERT

Sandstone writing tablets
strewn haphazardly over this
white desert and I
reach down and pick them
up one by one, looking
for answers that are not
there or have been erased
by wind and rain and
the slow sliding of desert
creatures, dumb to their
destruction of messages
that might have given a clue.

ADOBE INN

In this yellow Indian
room I try to sleep
knowing tomorrow will
determine nothing.
Even though I'm terrified
I like to think if things
don't work out, I'll leave.
Leave for what?
There is no safety.
There is only fear
becoming courage
in action.

LANDSCAPE AND A TRADER

The land was always there. Even now in his memory beneath the soil he can see the cottonwoods and the small clump of tules where the spring-fed arroyo runs through the red clay. In the morning when the red sun burst over the piñon trees on top of the mesa, he would whip back the Navajo blanket that served as cover and bedspread and walk to the door of his adobe home. And the land would be there. In the evening when he closed the trading post, and headed back to his one-room house, the land would be there. He would feel at peace that there was something that remained, permanent, patient, unchanging.

He was the only trader within forty miles. His trading post was like a hub of a great wagon wheel that brought Indians in from every point of the rim.

When he died, only the land witnessed his departure, and it was quiet, and said nothing. He was buried behind the post near the spot where the spring fed the little stream of red water that trickled through the silent land.

No one else came to run the trading post. There is only rubble there now. The spring is dried up and no marker remains over his grave. He and the land are one now. Only occasional flash floods and little wind twisters disturb the arroyo, and the windswept land says nothing. It is only there as it always was. And he sees it above him and he is happy.

CHILDHOOD MEMORIES

I.

Every little boy should have a grandfather. When I was a little boy, I had a grandfather who wasn't really a grandfather; anyway that's what everybody said. But I knew he was my grandfather, even though my parents didn't know him, and he lived on the other side of the tracks and he was an Indian. Everyone called him Medicine Man and that always brought to my seven-year-old mind rows and rows of aspirin bottles that I imagined he gave to all the sick people in the world.

I first met my grandfather at the Santa Fe train station in Gallup. He had long gun-gray hair which he kept tied up in a neat little ball on the back of his head, and he sold turquoise rings to tourists who stopped at the Fred Harvey House to stretch their legs whenever the El Capitan or the Chief or Grand Canyon Limited stopped in Gallup. Grandfather was always there, his rings spread out on a Navajo rug, his back propped against the beige stucco wall of the depot.

My mother worked all day in the laundry behind the depot and my daddy worked all day on an island in the South Pacific. He was a marine sergeant and wore long shiny medals for marksmanship. My grandfather was my daytime companion and friend and I sat for long hours after school, when the other kids were playing, and talked with my grandfather, the medicine man.

It was always warm sitting on the rug next to my grandfather. He would tell me about Corn Woman and Pollen Boy and Bluebird and how the Navajos, whom he always called *Dine'*, the people, came out of the belly of the earth. My whole childhood was filled with stories and pictures, the odor of raw blanket wool and the low quiet tones of my grandfather's voice.

II.

I take up my pen,
and I remember.
I reach down deep inside
for the feel of things
the way they were.
I smell again the sagebrush,
and I taste the piñon,
and I hear the trains
coughing into Gallup.
A small boy, five years old,
is holding a Daisy B-B gun.
He is standing by
a little brick house
on Aztec Avenue.
It is December 7, 1941.
The war begins.

III.

Trains rumble through my childhood
squealing and steaming and grunting up
speed, their melancholy groans sooting
my world with ashes of now.
I used to stand on the Harvey House
platform looking before and after,
longing to jump onto a train
and watch the coal dust blow
behind me as I stood in the engine
cab, arm on the window, my right
hand jerking squirts of whistle
before me, clearing the tracks,
heralding eternal comings and goings,
leaving ashes settling forever
on the concrete slabs of passing
railroad platforms.

IV.

There was a boy's sip of apricot brandy in the
back seat as we drove back from rabbit hunting.
It wasn't always snowing, but there was always
snow on the ground, and you were glad you had
on thick woolen socks and leather boots with
plenty of neat's-foot oil rubbed into them.
Rabbits were plentiful then. You didn't get that
awful, sorry feeling you get now when you spot
one lonely rabbit shivering inside a clump of sage,
waiting for your finger on the trigger. It was
more like you were doing nature a favor by

thinning out the rabbits and bringing home
scores of cottontails that would keep the family
going all winter if they were dressed right and
put down in the freezer in good packing.

Usually, we went to San Mateo for our rabbits
because that's where they were. Anyway, that's
what dad said, and I never doubted him when it
came to hunting.

V.

Empty balloon,
inner tube discarded
in a corner of the room
where we worked, half-hearted,
on Saturday mornings to earn
enough for the movies in the afternoon.

Still in the corner, still helpless for air
poor inner tube, flattened balloon,
I never noticed you back there
when I was a boy of June.
I see you now and
scream for air.

VI.

I remember the last tune
I danced. I was thirteen
and the dance was a farewell
for me and I danced with

the mother of my childhood sweetheart
who never knew she was my girl.
And then the dance was over
until now. I remember, and
I want to dance again. I
realize I am nearing forty.
No trauma, really. I just want
to dance. In more ways than one
I want to dance—to make up
for something, to be going again.
So I run to the altar with a tan.

VII.
When, in the windswept childhood
of my desert days, I saw my heart,
etched on the sandhills, blowing away,
I did what I could to befriend the wind.
And now, when the sound of the wind
beckons me, I return to sandhills
to see how much of my heart remains
outlined on the face of the red rocks
standing sentinel at the edge of town.

III. sea animals

Poetry is the journal of a sea animal living on land, wanting to fly the air.

— Carl Sandburg

... one painting shook me above all. It was as though I had seen it for the first time .... Numerous fish were cruising in the water with lifted tails, frolicking happily, whereupon a flying fish in their midst suddenly spread its little fins, took a leap and bounded out of the sea in order to breathe air. Too big for its slavish piscine nature it was, too big to live all its life in water. It suddenly longed to transcend its destiny, breathe free air, and become a bird—for a flash only, as long as it could endure. But that was enough; this flash was eternity. That is the meaning of eternity.

— Nikos Kazantzakis

I begin again: to try and set it down in words that remember how the weather was and how the people talked and how the wind blew. I reach around corners for things, tangible objects to latch onto. The things and the people are sometimes fictions, the memories are not, or so I pretend. And in pretending, they become more real than if they really happened.

To Herbert Lomas

SEA ANIMALS

I am
white dolphin
leaping high
from deep water.
With winged fin
I try to fly.

I am
black otter
playing fish,
sliding down in
winter wish
toward my origin.

RETREAT

You do what you
can when you're trapped
this way, shipwrecked
on an island
of your own making.
You grow accustomed to
the geography you've mapped
out in flight and select
a further highland
retreat suited to shaking
off fear and you try
not to search the sky.

THE PURGATIVE WAY

When the heart hears,
the ears are silent.
When the mind sees,
the eyes are blind.
When the will obeys,
eyes and ears are opened,
and the mind plays.

PILGRIM I.

When on a foggy February day
like today
I try to say sincerely
that I love you,
it all comes out misty
and clouded
and full of phelgm.
I reach through fog to you,
but even with headlights
at low beam
the soupy sickness between us
blurs my vision
and I pass you by
in a fine mist of pain.
The roadsigns read obscure towns
and they sizzle out of sight
behind my speeding flight
away from you in my haste
to find you.

PILGRIM II.

You reach out, trying to find
some point of contact
with God.
You know he is reaching down
to you
but your hands miss each other
somewhere
in the darkness.
The darkness is your own
and you look, cat-eyed,
through the night
for him who is
light.
You feel him all around you
and inside you
but somehow you fail
to meet.

Then you reach out to some stranger
on a crowded bus
and your hand feels
God's grip
and his light shines in your eyes
and you hear his
human voice.

DULWICH VILLAGE, ENGLAND

This lovely chapel that I must explore,
this strong Anglican door,
this quiet of a time out of place,
of a pace Elizabethan
in the heart of modern London . . . .
As soon as I enter
quiet stills my heart, as if
some stabilizing rhythm
has synchronized its quaking.
My whole self hums
with a serene past that is quiet
because it is no more.
It was not quiet when Burbage lived
in Dulwich Village.
The present
is tense with presence;
absent, the past is still.

CROSSING THE CHANNEL

I missed the sea this year, except
from the air,
the crossed plank of my plane
casting its shadow across the white cliffs
of Dover, and then
wrinkling across the Channel to Calais.
Why are we always
skimming quickly
over those things we love?
I should have parachuted
while I had the chance;
but we always land
before I can jump.

FRAU

In a cafe
in Paris I heard
you laugh, old
German frau. How
you laughed above
the noise of all the
talking crew of tourists.
Laugh on, old woman;
I turned and saw
the pain in your eyes;
laugh on, I understand,
laugh on, to keep
back the tears.

ALLEY

You come at last
to that dead end
You've been running toward
all your life.
No more
doors to open,
no more
strength for climbing.
You turn
and face your pursuers
and there is
no one there.
The bare alley behind
is loud
with the echoes
of your own fears.
It's a long walk back.

CLASSROOM

The desks were all different
when I was fourteen.
They were facing the other wall
and Father Hyacinth sat at a desk
that rested on a podium
so that even when he was sitting,
you had to look up.
Now I sit at the teacher's desk
and it rests on the floor.
I look out at these freshmen
taking my *Julius Caesar* test
and I can't remember the way
it was with me when I was fourteen.
I remember so much, down to
the glasses I wore, but I can't
remember how it was.
The view from these windows
hasn't changed at all,
but the feel of it has.
Something changes
at the back of the eye,
some inner interpreter,
a memory, another I.

BLACKBIRDS

In early March
when the wind whips the trees
outside my chilly room,
I walk to the window
and look west into the sunset.

I'm searching for the blackbirds
that I know will rise
from our neighbor's field,

swarms of birds
pelleting the gray sky,
seeking the bore of their origin,
gun barrel
of their beginning.

RELEASE

To look at trees outside
your window and the glide
of hawks on wing above
draws you out and love
is possible again. Self-
centering kills the elf
and puts demons inside
the mind. You must ride
somewhere out there or
you die inside the door.

MONDAY

last notes of
the black harp
are playing
through the
winter trees,
and three crows
clump up
and pump away,
their music
silent, gray

MINORITY

Little things like chickadees
and titmice, and trees
just beginning to bud
and cows chewing cud
and juncos on a white field
make the heart stop and yield
to tiny divinity revealed.

FOR LEO NIETO
(1936-1973)

July and I
  turn again
    to the little stuccoed house on Fifth Street
    and the single row of beans I planted there
    outside the window where you whistled
    for me to come out and play;

    to the Colorado fishing trip
    where you leaned near the trout swift water
    and caught those grand tugs
    only a boy of twelve is proud of;

    to the car wreck on the Ramah Road
    when you were spared the tumbling
    over at high speed and I was

almost there but backed out
because we hadn't told our
parents we were going;

to that other trip you didn't take
when I left Gallup, Greyhound bound
for a future you were not a part of
and from which I never really returned.

And now July and I
  read of you
    leaning by the troutless Pacific
    your last line tugged down, bound
    for a present I am not a part of
    and from which you will not return.

NOTES FOR THOMAS MERTON

storm over Gethsemani
   and dead leaves flying
lightning crackling
   above your grave
a dry storm
   with painful droplets
      of heavy water
flung into my face

then the sudden dying
   and the steady streams
      of wet rain
far into the night
   as the monks sleep

and I, awake,
   tasting the cool Siloe-breeze

pushed by the thunder
and I, awake,
    feeling your bones
        crackling beneath my window
as thunder blasts
    the gentle chiming
        of the monastery clock

God speaks in the thunderstorm.

and the violence you deplored
    visits your grave
        raging at the passive sod
        raging at the green passive sod
at the black raging soil

GRAVE OF MARTIN LUTHER KING

uprooted body seeded here
   beneath this last lynching tree
      beside the red-brick Ebenezer
this bare tree
   rounding your grave
rhythms
   into the structure of his peace
a black form against the sky
   rooted deeply
      in the Georgia soil

WANDERER

I turn around
and hike down the streets
of all my years
of fears
and they are
shining-brightly sheets
of silver
where black asphalt
used to be,
and all the stuccoed houses
are alabaster
because I see you
walking beside me
where you always were
when I was blind
to see you.

RANDOM THOUGHTS

I.

I didn't
lift the receiver
though my hand trembled
at what I could have had.
I hope you love me for it.
Some would say
I was a fool—

II.

Lord
the penance of living
is mostly for loving
someone other than you.

III.

To say no
to everyone else
but you
(wanting to say yes)

makes me love you more
but others
more enticing
because they are at hand.

IV.

Young,
you ask forgiveness
for loving;
old,
for not.

V.

What will be telling
of my love when
I am gone?
This touch,
I hope,
this reaching out to heal.

BY THE SEA

I.

The discipline of listening,
of inspiration that comes
from sensitized nerve
endings, open to quiet!
The noise of silence
can kill you.

II.

Sitting in "The Village Zoo,"
Lauderdale watering place,
I read *The Nick Adams Stories*
leisurely over Lowenbrau
on tap and the first story
is Nick's fear of death
entitled, "Three Shots."
I order another beer,
a toast for Ernest, who
finally licked that fear,
but not the other.

III.

Life, after all, is a gift
for giving away. Once you
throw it from you and lift
your spirit up, nothing you do
matters quite so much as freedom from life returning again
and haunting you to be
someone instead of no one.

IV.

Everyone runs to the beach
frantically seeking the sun.
I hear the short fast screech
of tires, a signal that someone
has won a parking spot,
his own place of reference
for a few hours to blot
out the pain of defense,
the fatigue, the ache
of living in deference.

V.

Trying to avoid too much sun
I heap on suntan cream
and lie back on the sand, one
more day away to dream.
Memories of sun never help much
when the beach is far behind,
and I return to the rough touch
of life. This day, though, is kind;
that's all I can stand—one day
of sun (or cloud) at a time.
No memories, no future, no way
to stay the fear but rhyme.

VI.

Suddenly here by the beach
I realize I am not an animal
of the sea. My longest reach
is much too minimal.
Besides, the land ends always
at the water's edge. And I—
I'm through running away.
I stand here, facing the sky.

VII.

No beach nor sand can solve
anything, nor induce forgetfulness.
The wheels of the mind revolve;
nature, indifferent, more or less.

VIII.

On land
again looking
for a hand—
The sea
surrenders
more readily.

IV. man with a guitar

*Little stumbling poems make the time seem shorter
and the confusion less painful when we cannot
pray. If we were always lost in prayer, there would
be no need for poetry. For we don't need anything
else when God is totally present to us. But no one,
of course, is ever lost in prayer for any length of
time. We are in fact outside of time in true prayer,
only to return again to the merely human waiting,
searching, yearning for eternity. In those ticks
between the silences of eternity, poetry is born.*

*Poetry then is not only "the journal of a sea
animal, living on land, wanting to fly the air," it is
also the journal of a sea animal, living on land,
remembering that he has flown.*

To Fr. Andrew Fox and all my Franciscan brothers

AUTUMN SONG

If you are not here
when the trees turn red
and the crisp Canadian breeze
blows through our woods,
I will walk the leaves down
thinking of you and how you
made the dark seasons light
though your heart sank low
in winter's grip. And then I'll
lift my eyes to the sky and
sing a bright autumn song for you.

ABSENCE

I stand in the warm woods
shivering,
the sun streaming
through the red leaves
onto my chill.
The sun cannot replace you
who walked these woods down
with me.
The woods are crimson now
and all our summer's green
is dying.
I lift my eyes to heaven
but my feet are cold and still,
unable to walk
alone,
remembering absence.

MAN WITH A GUITAR

I.

I play the guitar now.
Something happened inside
to make that possible,
to make me want to play
at age thirty-eight what
I never had time for
at age eighteen with
all the time I needed.
Perhaps your youth
pursues you until you
yield and do what
you should've done
when time was for
worry and wasting on
things you know now
would have been better
off left alone.

II.

I wonder what they'd say,
those young singers,
if they knew I too now play
a rough tune with fingers
clumsy from years of holding
pencils and chalk and cigar
warm to the touch! Folding
my hands, I pray that they are
happy I've grown young enough
again to sing and play the stuff
of youth, the happy kind,
to scare away the goblins of the mind.

III.

When there is no time
to practice your guitar

and you've forgotten how far
away the north star is,
and there is no gentle rhyme
to soothe your shattered nerves,
it's time to make your life your
own again.

IV.

Sounds other than this tune
surround my heart and play
upon my spirit from beyond.
Or are these silent sounds
inside the melodies I hear?
I only know that playing
songs to hear releases music
for another, inner ear.

AWAKENING

I have lost the leisure to write.
"Lost" is perhaps the wrong word
because circumstances and people
have stolen the little time I had left
for thinking and penning words
onto paper. And I cannot rest until
I regain those lost lands of my mind.
The geography of my own heart I must
somehow reclaim before the seven
evil spirits enter there and find
my imagination abandoned and empty.
Time and space unclaimed is never neutral.

MYRTLE BEACH

I remember now,
here by the ocean in South Carolina,
my eighth grade class
because my English teacher
in junior high
was from this then so distant place
I never dreamed
of seeing.
And my teacher jumps into my mind
young as he was
and not
twenty-five years older
as he is now
wherever he is, here or hereafter.
The wonder of memory that stops time
and is never altered
unless
the senses perceive the present
and shatter eternity with their truth!

CHILDHOOD

I took you for granted
when we played cowboys
together and acted out
the movies we saw.
It wasn't till we
quit acting and left
for the unreal world
beyond the sandlot
that I realized . . .

JEREMIAH'S LAMENT

I should never
have feared losing
you forever.
It's not my choosing
but yours to sever
this old bruising
called love. Never
will you stop musing
over my wounds!
There'll be war tunes
for us enough
and some rough
epitaph of how
we had our row
together.

FRANCIS

You, my Father Francis,
I seek you in every cave
and lonely place of Umbria.
I listen for your voice
in a sudden wind or
surprising shaft of light,
realizing all the while
that you will come
in some poor brother
whom I meet along the way.
I see him (you) in my
pilgrim's eye. He comes
like me searching for you
and something more, I'm sure.

AGING

O how they dig deep, the years.
How they furrow our lives
with plows of laughter and tears.
I read their passage in the lines
of your face, my friend.
And I remember the years
that left those creases there,
and how it was with us through
all that time of sowing and
reaping we shared together.
We are open fields now
and life slides through us
like old, familiar ground.

AUTHORITY

And who will provide answers
for us in all those decisions
we've made for others, incisions
in the heart by lancers
inept with problems of the heart?
We operate because others
more skilled have feared to,
and our own clumsiness smothers
us and makes us wonder how true
we've been in our forced part.
Lord, forgive us our operations
upon your people; the stations
of your cross we repeat and
play too many parts unplanned.

MENTAL WARD

How do we hear the music
when all the voices die
that let us hear, here
in the comfortable room
where few really care
enough to let us listen?
We grow deaf through fear
and cannot hear the
music or the silence.
For fear is the opposite
of music here where we
hear only with permission.
We are the silent ones who
only listen, and now that
too is taken from us. Ay!
We scream in silence,
throats forbidden to cry.

V. the ascent of mount subasio

I haven't yet found a way to say what I know, what I have learned. It has something to do with recognizing God's mysterious plan in everything that happens in our lives. How do you say that without seeming banal, without clichés? The answer is somewhere inside, in the geography of the unconscious mind, in what I seem to have forgotten. I reach for the symbol, the image deep inside, and Mount Subasio rises in my soul.

I take you by the hand, Mary, my Lady, and I begin the ascent of this holy mountain. Where will you lead me, woman, feminine side of my life in the Lord? You see, I didn't know before you took me by the hand.

To my mother and father

DREAM WOMAN

Lady of my woods,
the path to you
cuts across
all my desires
and enters the sanctuary
of secluded oaks
swiftly
beneath my feet

I look
for your reflection
in the little stream
that runs beneath
the bridge we built
to watch your image by

And always just
below the silver surface

of this trysting creek
shining coyly
back at me
are you,
Mary, Virgin,
lady of my woods

And turning around
to surprise you
at my shoulder,
I see only
a face of moon

Again in stillness
you have eluded me
as you slip away
racing deeper
inside my woods

LINDEN TREE

December snow falling
wet upon the gray branches
of my linden tree.
I reach again for you
who send this snow
to remind me
of everything that falls
from above.
My eyes turn heavenward
and I am freed
from my horizontal world.
Poetry looks up
where you dwell and
brings you to earth again.
You rise above the earth
and fall again and again
for us who forget you are here
where we walk and talk and
live our hollow lives.

WATERFOWL

Always the same
when, in this wintering into spring
the ducks and geese
fly the cold skies northward
and I wonder will they freeze?
They seldom do, it seems.
Unlike man they know enough
to feel the thaw beneath the ice,
to see buds upon barren branches.

FEBRUARY MORNING

Two birds clumped together
high in that single oak towering
even with my third floor window.
Slate sky and landscape
and all out of doors gray
with waiting for spring . . . Even
those two little clumps of bird
seem shaky this February morning.
I look up from my writing pad
and they are gone and the tree
is balanced and symmetrical again.

LENT

You see us begin again
with ashes that have lost something
on modern man who washes well.
We are too antiseptic to wear ashes
through all the forty days of soil.
And so we reach for clean ways
of growing seeds sterile with piety.

EASTER

Out of sight, behind
the scrub oak, bounding
away from me, the hind
runs on, silver pounding
hooves flashing bright
in my lonely night
of fear.

    I cry out for
you to wait for me,
but there is nothing more
than this trembling tree,
streaming the linen crepe
of your white escape.

WOUNDED SPARROW

Alone again
with only the wind
and one lone sparrow
singing into the cold.
I reach into the night
and you are there
to take me back.
You are faithful,
you hear the cry
of the wounded sparrow.

MEDALS

The medals
that hang helplessly
around our necks
are fashioned
of the gold of tears
and good-byes.

POETRY

In this constant craft,
this trying over and again
to make words sing,
I find redemption.
The word becomes flesh
in the word multiplied
and juxtaposed and edited
and erased and rejected
and sometimes dying
and rising from the tomb.
The page is my parish
and words my people.
At times we break into song.

HOLINESS

Holiness is
the music of God's movement
within us,
stretching every note
beyond our hearing.

LOVE

Something we failed to do
a long, long time ago
comes back to haunt us who
think the past lets go.
We love early or late
but love we will, despite
how hard we try to simulate
indifference to nature's right.

INDIRECTIONS

I write late into the night
and drink tea and wait
for solutions to flow from my pen.
(I used to think I might
really find reasons straight
from God and utter Amen.)
But now I pray and write
and wait for indirections
that straighten into directions.
A truer solution, a better Amen.

MADONNA PIETA

Who are you, Mary,
child and broken man
upon your knee?
Both baby and man agree
that you are all-woman,
life-giver,
lady of dreams and roses.
Youth pines that you are
purity unreachable,
and age proclaims
you fertility-fulfilled,
one perfect act
of will—surrender
to Motherhood—
childing you
forever with God.
Man-ing your womb is he,
the first-born of many
to share divinity
through virgin birth,
humanity, by lying heavy,
broken in your open lap.

ASSISI

Study I

A saffron sky across the west,
Assisi splashed with light like
catches of Villa Lobos in stone.
I sit alone and watch the sun
play upon these ancient walls.
Night falls quickly in September.

Study II

Sunrise in Assisi,
before the noisy motorbikes
rattle the town awake.
I try to freeze this "still"
in my imagination.
The reel speeds up
as soon as motorcars
start coughing.

Study III

Morning chill in the air,
autumn is blowing through the valley,
freeing the summer mist
that chokes the Umbrian plain;
cold, damp winter clears its throat.

ASSISI MOON

The moon I see
is crescent tonight.
But all its mystery
is lost upon my sight.
I am heavy with earth.

NIGHT OF THE TOWER
(Francis of Assisi)

That night of the tower
that night in lonely Rome
heart feeling far from home,
you cried out in your hour
of anguish that even you
were afraid to be alone.
Then, Francis, light shone
from you bright and true;
you were one of us,
one of the quiet, lonely souls
for whom the stars are holes
in the sky signifying emptiness.
The barren Roman moon
became your Sister then,
a woman far from men
and farther from peopled noon.
We made you our own,
a fellow-sufferer that night
of the tower when you might
have uttered nothing, or thrown
away your humanity by
praying a lovely lie.

THE GARDEN

I.

The mountain fails me tonight
and the moon and the stars of Subasio
are powerless because you are gone.
The white beams on the stone bench are cold.
I wonder where you are and what moon
you see and if you are alone like me.
The familiar sounds of the garden scare me;
will we have to find its innocence again?
In the shivering cypresses I wait for dawn.

II.

Oh, yes, I will wait the sun's rising
and cry into the rain of forgetfulness,
the rain that falls from cloudless skies.

III.

With the taste of dawn in my mouth
I remember the mellow mornings
when we would wake and smile
into the boredom of others' eyes.
We had so much to do
to bring up the sun in our lives.
Now the sun rises on its own
and the taste of dawn is sour.

HEALING

Once again out of the chaos,
the word.
I pick up my pen
and begin.
Always there is the distance
between the experience
and the word,
time helping the act
to find its expression.

CIMABUE'S FRANCIS
(Basilica, Assisi)

In those sad eyes
happy with their open stare,
the light mirroring the seer,
I see me, and you are transparent,
so little in your homeliness
as your pointed ears gather
the pixiness of your spirit.

Francis, little one,
clinging to the plaster
in this dark corner
of Brother Elias' monument,
who would ever think
to look for you
here in this dark corner
of the lower church?
You surprised me,
bent as you are
by the curve of the arch
supporting the upper church
of this incongruous Basilica.
You look even shorter
with the weight of all that stone
upon your slender neck.
I wonder
why your hands are fixed
in that awkward position?

THE ASCENT OF MOUNT SUBASIO

I. Assisi Rain

Place your warm lips
upon my dry heart
and pray for clean,
September rain.
The brown mantle
of my love
surrounds you.

II. Rocca Maggiore

The poppies weep in the red fields,
the blood of their tears a red mosaic
on the plain below the Rocca Maggiore.
And I remember "Blessingway,"
those poems without color,
too barren even for transparent tears.

III. Cliff

With your wet words washing my hearing
and the light birds, the ginestra, clearing
my vision, I think about the white beach

and the long, final drink before my reach
for the blue mountain, Subasio.

IV. Carceri

You have become wet violets
in the dark woods
by the secret cave.
You are their taste,
the color of their surprises.

VI. Summit

The ceremonies of our endless partings,
with the incense turning acrid in the wind,
with the candles running wet
onto the little altars beside the bed
and we keeping back the sacrificial tears,
holding this liturgy against despair.
Oh, love, we must believe
in some future ceremony of joy
where the blue incense of our purity
will rise toward accepting heaven
and the candles will warm the room
and the painful altars where we prayed
will catch responsible tears of joy.

FRANCIS OF ASSISI

I. Conversion

Before his illness,
before the event that changed their names,
they were outside, the people and the things.
Afterwards,
they lived inside his heart:
sickness brings indoors the outside world,
the names changed
by walking an inner garden
with God at your side.

The illness fell upon him suddenly
though he had seen it coming
during those long days in prison
when he wore the mask of joviality.
He would look up afraid,
feeling the heaviness descending.
Then the coming home to Assisi,
seeing the pain in his parents' eyes,

and lying alone
in the helpless bed.
He closed his eyes,
and everything
building up for years
fell through the tiles
and he surrendered himself
to the dark coma of evil.

The emptiness,
the fear that it would never end,
and the terrible weakness unto death.
The long days of night
and the terror of the dry mouth
hollow of spirit and life.
He lay there for a year,
a boy alone facing the void.

He walks through the poppies
below the city walls,

a child of the garden outdoors.
His bed has turned to flowers
red with his rising.

II. The Leper

Those long nights in bed
sick and delirious with self
he sees his devils
and embraces them one by one,
repulsive because they are his own.
And then he lets them go,
surrendering them to the depths,
he thinks, in self-forgiveness.

Then the day on the road
when he sees himself in the leper.
There they are again
manned before him,
and he shudders.

Once again the embrace,
and they are gone.
He surrenders to love
those spirits of his own making.
Love kills the devils
who hate us.
Love figures the disfigured
and heals the mind
and its diseased eyes.
Now he sees angels everywhere.

The leper trembles
in their passing
and Francis trembles
feeling them flee.
Fear of shaking
holds man enthralled.
Shake them loose, he cries,
and all creation shivers

and dies peacefully at his feet.
He now walks unshod
feeling the soft, redeemed dirt
kissing his soles.

III. The Stigmata

He returns to the valley of Spoleto,
the man seraphic charged with fire.
Everything is as it was
except that now he sees it all
through open wounds,
and everything is dearer
because it costs so much to see it.
When you see through wounds,
the color of your pain
changes the colors of the world.

She is there,
Clare of the golden tower,

gold since forever became a wound.
He stops at San Damiano
in his journey from the mystic mountain,
and he will have a hut there
that she has made for him of broken twigs.
She is there,
her golden hair cut close beneath her veil,
walking silently into the rat rich room.
She kneels by his side,
ointments of healing in her hand.
And there in the shadows
she touches softly his bleeding eyes,
her tears falling warm onto his cheeks.
He is home.

Fifty days in the shade of the earth
with Clare daily by his side.
All light is painful,
except the light that is Clare,
there in the dark of his wooden cave.

Then at the end
wombed again from the earth,
he stands up alone
legs shaking with wet
and salutes the light with a canticle:
"All praise be yours, my Lord,
Through all that you have made,
And first my Lord Brother Sun,
Who brings the day . . ."
And he leaves the cave,
the stone rolling back before him.

Now his wounds are lightings.
He sees again with the illumination of God
his hands ray the Risen Christ,
his side probes the human heart
with soft October light,
his feet warm the cold Assisi stones.
He has risen from the dead.

Murray Bodo is a Franciscan priest and poet. After his ordination in 1964 he earned a master's degree in English from Xavier University in Cincinnati, then served as spiritual director and head of the English Department at St. Francis Seminary, Cincinnati, and Duns Scotus College, Detroit. Father Murray presently teaches English at Chatfield College, Brown County, Ohio, and is on the staff of St. Anthony Messenger Press. During the summer he lives in Assisi, Italy, where he is a staff member and lecturer for a program of Franciscan renewal.

Also by Murray Bodo, O.F.M.:

Francis: The Journey and the Dream
Clare: A Light in the Garden
Walk in Beauty: Meditations from the Desert
Song of the Sparrow: Meditations and Poems to Pray by
The Song of St. Francis (double-cassette album)